Bible Based Cognitive Behavioral Therapy

Using the Bible and CBT to Manage Depression, Fear, and Anxiety

Joyce Nyirenda, M.A., LCMHC

TTL Publishing

Wake Forest, North Carolina

Bible Based Cognitive Behavioral Therapy by Joyce Nyirenda, M.A., LCMHC
TTL Publishing
P.O. Box 1744
Wake Forest, North Carolina 27588
info@tokunbotheleader.com
Visit the publisher's website at tokunbotheleader.com.

Cover design by Loughlin Design.

Visit the author's website at jpnconsultants.com.

Unless otherwise noted, all scriptures are taken from the New King James Version or English Standard Version of the Bible.

ISBN: 978-1-7378576-1-7

CONTENTS

I have thought long and hard about how the Bible can be brought into Cognitive Behavioral Therapy (CBT), or rather how we can use the teachings of the Bible in CBT. As a licensed clinical mental health counselor, Cognitive Behavioral Therapy is one of my go-to treatments to care for clients. The basis for Cognitive Behavioral Therapy is that if we can change our cognitions, (thoughts or cognitive processes such as our core beliefs, perceptions, attitudes, expectations, and our problem-solving ability), we can change our behavior (Beck, 1964).

CBT was founded in 1964 by Dr. Aaron Beck. Dr. Beck was a psychiatrist who treated patients with anxiety and depression, among other things. In his early days, Dr. Beck stated, "CBT is a model based on the hypothesis that our emotions, our body responses, and behaviors are determined by how we see, view or understand what has taken place (event or situation) (Beck, 1964). In other words, the events and situations that take place around us and in our lives cause us to respond in a certain way based on our thought contents, beliefs, perceptions, and so forth. What this means is that an event or a situation (also known as an antecedent or trigger) in and of itself does not make us respond in any particular way. It is our thought process in relation to or our perception of the event that makes us respond in a particular manner. (3)

Dr. Beck further asserted that,

"CBT is based on the belief that thought distortions and maladaptive thought processes (which he also referred to as schema or schemata) play a role in the development and

maintenance of psychological disorders, and that symptoms and associated distress can be reduced by teaching new information-process skills and coping mechanics" (4) Beck,' A. T. (1964)

What the preceding means is that a situation by, and in itself, cannot cause us distress; rather it is the way in which we interpret the situation that causes us to feel distressed. Our interpretation of an event or situation (antecedent or trigger) is determined by our cognitions, or the content of our thought processes, our core beliefs, and so on. These beliefs, thought processes, and cognitions are sometimes called automatic thoughts. These automatic thoughts are responsible for influencing our feelings, body responses, and behaviors. It is important for us to pay attention to our automatic thoughts because how a situation is interpreted is how we will automatically respond to the situation or event. What is seen by others reflects the contents of our thoughts or our cognitions. We can get an idea of someone's thought content by the way they respond to situations. This explains how different people can respond to or react to the same exact situation in entirely different ways.

The idea that our interpretation of events is governed by our perception of the situation and our interpretation is determined by our cognitions, is what made me believe that we could use the Word of God to change our core beliefs. If we could use the Word of God to change our responses to depressive and anxiety-provoking situations, then we could be changed for the better. The process of thought monitoring, thought stopping, and thought-replacement would help Believers if they replaced their core beliefs with the Word of God!

Studying and using Philippians 4:6-8 for years even before learning about CBT became a clear example of the CBT model for me. The more I used the words of verses 6 and 7 the clearer it became to me that this was a thought monitoring and replacement process. It will be explained in further detail later in the text how adding verse 8 completes the CBT model.

It is my hope that you will prayerfully seek to understand how to apply the various verses provided in the text to situations and examples given. This will help with managing or completely reducing the occurrence of depressive and anxiety provoking thoughts. As these anxious and depressive thoughts are reduced, ideally your feelings and behaviors towards situations that bring the onset of anxiety and depression will be altered. This text will delineate how using God's word and CBT strategies of thought monitoring, challenging your thoughts, and replacing them with God's word can help reduce or completely eradicate the occurrence of those three mental health issues in our lives.

It is important that one understands the difference between mental health and mental illness. This book is aimed at helping in managing or controlling mental health symptoms, which are usually milder than mental illness symptoms. Mental illness would be beyond the scope of this book and anyone with mental illness needs to contact their primary care doctor, a psychiatrist, or a mental health therapist for proper management of their symptoms. By mental illness I am referring to any condition that involves more than temporary depressive thoughts, worry or fear. Occasional anxiety is an expected part of life, such as feeling anxious for an upcoming exam, meeting or making an important decision and so forth. A mental health illness or disorder "does not go away and can get worse over time. The symptoms can interfere with daily activities such as job performance, relationships and schoolwork" (Nimh.nih,gov/health/topics/anxiety-disorders/index.shtm)

This book is not intended as a replacement for medical consultation. If your depressive and anxiety symptoms (which usually end up causing fear if unmanaged) are affecting your relationships or your ability to function on your job and/or school, you need to seek medical attention. One can continue to apply God's word as a tool in changing one's core beliefs while receiving medical attention. There is nothing wrong with applying medical help and the Word of God to help you heal.

CHAPTER ONE

The Power of Processing Your Thoughts

As we focus on using CBT as a tool or technique to change our core beliefs using God's word, there are several other definitions of CBT that need to be highlighted. In an article on, DeploymentPsych.org, it is stated that CBT for Depression (CBT.D) CBT is, "...a structured, short term, present-oriented approach to psychotherapy that helps patients modify unhelpful patterns of thinking and behavior in order to resolve current problems' (Deployment Psych.org).

It is also defined as: "CBT is a "problem focused" and "action-oriented" form of therapy that is geared at treating specific issues connected to a mental health disorder diagnosis" (www.academyofct.org).

Finally, CBT is an example of one type of psychotherapy (talk therapy) that can help people with anxiety disorders...it teaches people different ways of thinking, behaving and reacting to anxiety-producing and fearful objects and situations." (Nimh.nih.gov/health/topics/anxiety-disorders/index.shtm)

According to Dr. Aaron Beck and others who proposed the CBT model, this is how the cognitive model would look like in a diagram:

Diagram A

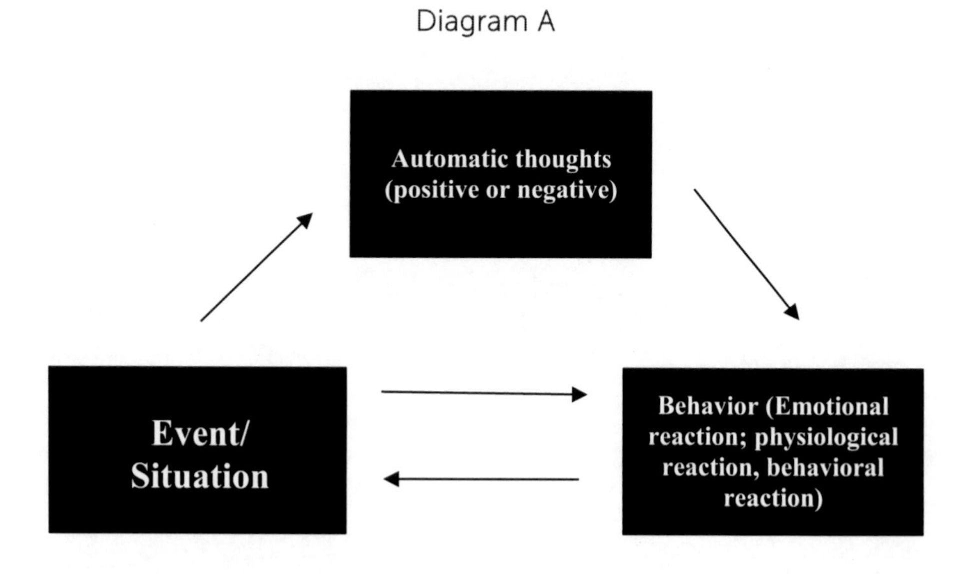

Behavior encompasses all our emotional, physiological and behavioral actions instead of behavior only displayed outwardly, and it can come out as positive behavior (in which our responses to the event are considered "acceptable" or "normal") or negative behavior.

Here is an example of how a situation would play out resulting in a positive response or behavior and a negative response or behavior.

You are waiting for a bus at a bus stop and another passenger approaches the bus stop, but while he is waiting, he is talking to himself.

There are two different reactions that you can have to this event.

A) First Reaction: Your thoughts are saying, "Oh my goodness, what am I going to do? He looks crazy. He is talking to himself. There is no one else here. Is he going to talk to me? Is he going to hurt me?"

Based on this thought process, you will probably become scared (emotional response), your heart might start racing or your palms may get sweaty (physiological response), and you may decide to leave and get away from the person (behavioral response).

B) Second Reaction: Your thoughts are saying, "Hmmmmm, it looks like he is talking to himself or maybe he is singing" in which case you may think. "Oh, that's normal, I have done that before,"

Based on this thought process, you may feel comfortable about the situation (emotion); you may smile at the individual (physiological response), and you may possibly try to talk to the person (behavior).

The responses to the exact same situation, by the same exact individual, differed based on how the individual interpreted or perceived the event/situation. CBT emphasizes that it is how an individual ***perceives*** an event or situation that dictates how they react to it, **not the event itself**. Based on the individual's automatic thoughts, one reaction was negative and the other reaction was positive.

In the example above, if the individual was distracted by something else, say talking to a friend who was there with her, she may not have noticed the stranger approaching. In that case, there would have been no response at all, since she would not have seen the stranger's "weird" behavior that caused her to react the way she did in the first example.

Cognitive Behavioral Therapy's A-B-C Model

What has been described above regarding the CBT model is sometimes also described as the A-B-C model. The A-B-C model is a slightly different form of the original CBT model (as shown in diagram A) that focuses on the relationship or connection that exists between our thoughts, feelings and behaviors. The A-B-C model looks like this:

1. A= Antecedent (trigger or activating event)
2. B= Behaviors/Beliefs
3. C= Consequences

Using our same bus stop example, the individual's responses would be reported as follows:

- **Antecedent/trigger/activating event**: Individual sees an approaching passenger talking to himself.
- **Behaviors/Beliefs:** Individual begins to think, "What is he going to do to me? He looks crazy. Will he hurt me?" These are the thoughts based on the individual's beliefs about people who talk to themselves. At this point, one can begin to see the person's behaviors such as being restless.
- **Consequences**: He either leaves the scene (because he believes the individual is crazy and may hurt him). The other consequence is that he stays there and smiles at him, almost tempted to strike a conversation with him because he believes nothing is wrong with him.

Diagram B

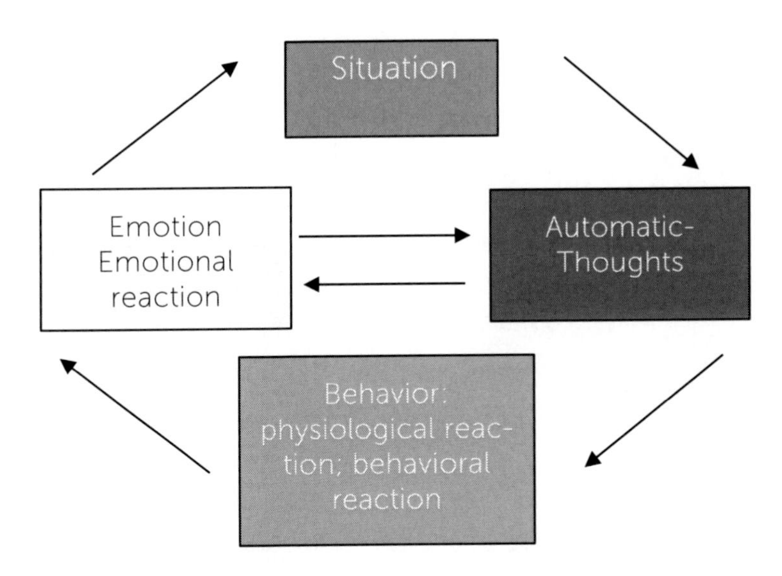

No matter which model of CBT is applied, we can be sure that the treatment model focuses on identifying an event which then leads to thought processes or beliefs which are eventually displayed in the ensuing behaviors.

CBT's Core Assumptions

According to, The Comprehensive Clinician's Guide to Cognitive Behavioral Therapy by Leslie Sokol, one of CBT's core assumptions is that:

Cognitive processes (our thoughts) influence emotions (how we feel) and behaviors; (How we respond or react to a situation, be it physically or physiologically). As such, the purpose of cognitive-behavioral interventions is to help individuals learn and acquire the skills to modify their cognitive set up (thought processes and core beliefs or their schemata) to come up with new behavioral skills and outcomes (Sokol, 2019).

Simply put, Cognitive Behavioral Therapy calls for individuals to learn how to change their way of thinking. Cognitive Behavior Therapy teaches people to modify (adjust) their belief system and to change their cognitive disposition (how they see things/events or even themselves). For a Christian, learning how to acquire the skills to modify one's cognitive set up, change one's way of thinking or how one sees themselves involves replacing old thought patterns and processes with God's word. In many cases, it may mean putting in God's word and getting rid of the lies and tales we have believed about God, the world, life and even ourselves.

Apostle Paul states, "And do not be conformed to this world, but be transformed by the renewing of your mind, that you may prove what is that good and acceptable and perfect will of God" (Rom. 12:2, NKJV). In this verse, we are told "...to be transformed by the renewing of our mind." Renewing is a present continuous verb, an action word that suggests something that is done repeatedly, or continuously. The process of being transformed is a continuous process. According to Apostle Paul, to change our thought process or the way we see things, we must regularly engage in the process of transforming our mind. Dictionary.com defines the word transform as, "...to change in form, appearance, or structure...to change in condition, nature or character, to convert etc.). Transformation calls for a change in form, appearance, or structure! In other words, the makeup, appearance or the structure of our mind must change, not only in its structure but its condition, it's nature or traits. It is important to understand that transformation is a process that involves the visible change in the structure of our brain (mind). When we allow our mind to be transformed, there will be an inevitable change in our behavioral, emotional and physiological responses to situations because the structure and composition of our mind has changed. The big takeaway here is that it is not only CBT that teaches us "...to acquire the skills to modify our cognitive set up," God's word encourages us to do the same as well. The difference is that in CBT we must learn various ways like thought monitoring, thought stopping, and thought replacement. However, the Bible teaches us to renew or change our thought processes by meditating on the Word of God.

Thought Monitoring, Thought Stopping, and Thought Replacing

There are many theories that have been proposed in assisting with changing one's cognitive disposition, their way of thinking, their core belief system, and their automatic thoughts. Among the most common ways to change the way we think is using thought monitoring, thought stopping and thought replacement. What this means is that an individual must take the responsibility of recognizing unproductive thoughts and stopping them before they lead to negative (unwanted) behavioral outcomes such as anxiety, fear, or depression. These mechanisms suggest that it is our responsibility to pay attention to what we are thinking about so that we can "catch" unproductive thoughts before they get to a place of turning into negative behaviors.

The idea of thinking about what we are thinking about or monitoring our thoughts may seem new or at best strange to a lot of us, but it is a particularly important process that we all need to become familiar with. We cannot change our thoughts or the content of our thought process if we do not pay attention to what we are thinking about. In CBT we say that the behaviors that we show on the outside are an indication of how we see, perceive, and think about what has happened (trigger or event) which leads to how we feel. It is important that we become active participants in our thought process. If we do not become active in monitoring our thoughts, we will continue to respond to situations around us without being actively involved in deciding how we should respond. The good news is that we can be actively involved in deciding how to respond to events and situations that take place around us. We can do this by following the thought monitoring, thought stopping and thought replacement process. In this model we are encouraged to pay attention to what is going on in our heads. We should constantly be asking ourselves: What am I thinking about? Are these good thoughts? Are my thoughts true? Who or what is the source of these thoughts? If we decide that our thoughts are not good, or not true, then we can choose not to agree with them. This is where the verse we discussed earlier on from Romans 12:2 comes in; we learn to transform our minds by renewing them. Part of renewing our minds happens during the process of monitoring our thoughts and discarding what is not good, Godly, or productive and replacing them with positive thoughts.

Another example to help expand on this topic could be a situation between what a parental figure may say to you and how it will impact your behavior. If your mother says something to you which makes you automatically feel like your mother does not love you, you may immediately begin to feel unloved by your mother. You may begin to think your mother prefers your sister to you and so forth. If you stay on this line of thought, what do you think you will feel towards your mother? Also, what do you think you will feel as your mother's child? It is at this point, that you have the choice to either continue thinking thoughts of how your mother does not love you or has never loved you or to tell yourself, "You know, maybe she was upset when she said that to me. Maybe she had too many things going on at that moment." Usually, when we allow ourselves to monitor our thoughts and choose a path of thinking that is different from our automatic thoughts, we win the battle of going into sadness, anxiety or even fear. If you decide that your mother was likely preoccupied with other things and she did not really mean what she said to you, you have just won a possible battle with a bout of depression, sadness, or feelings of not being wanted.

In a scenario, the idea of thought monitoring, thought stopping (which usually comes after we challenge our automatic thoughts) and thought replacement looks something like this:

Event/situation: Your mother says something to you that sounds as if she is saying she doesn't love you.

Automatic Thoughts: She doesn't love me; she loves my sister more; she would never say something like that to her.

Possible behavioral outcome: Sadness, anger outburst, withdrawal into your shell, and so on.

At this point, you can either go along with these negative thoughts or you can choose to challenge them. Challenging our thoughts simply means taking a serious look at what we are thinking and asking ourselves if what we are thinking about is true or if it is based on the fact that currently our feelings are hurt. When we allow ourselves to challenge our thought patterns instead of just going along with them, it gives us the opportunity to look at a situation differently and most likely to end up with a different and better perspective.

You should notice that at the point where you challenge your thought process, one side of your thought pattern tends to be negative and the other positive. Typically, negative thoughts end up producing negative behaviors. If you think your mother does not love you, which is a negative thought, you will most likely become sad or depressed. This in turn will show up in you having a somber mood toward your mother, not wanting to talk to her anymore, and/or isolating yourself. On the other hand, if you choose to look at things differently when you challenge your thoughts, you may end up thinking, "You know, that is not true, I know my mother loves me. She was probably just overwhelmed with something else when she said that to me." At that point, you will most likely feel relieved and get the feelings of being loved by your mother back again. This positive thought process produced positive behaviors and thinking patterns. Thinking positively led you to have the feeling of being loved or relieved which ultimately leads you to smiling and being yourself again. Therefore, it is important that we all learn how to challenge our thoughts. The process of challenging our thoughts happens when we take a moment to think about what we are thinking about and then seeing if our thoughts are true or not. Applying God's word to various situations also helps us with thinking positively. So, even if you are convinced that your mother does not love you, but you know what God's word says about how much He loves you, you may find peace and encouragement in that moment in His love. This may buy you time to rethink what you felt about your mother. You may remember what He says in Psalm 27:10, "When my father and mother forsake me, then the LORD will take me up."

In a diagram this process is represented by a triangle with "The Event" on the bottom left corner, "thought process" would be at the top of the triangle and the behavior at the bottom of the right angle. Remember, an event or situation (also known as an antecedent or trigger) is what causes us to start thinking about the issue and based on our thought process, our behavior follows. If we choose to go with the positive thoughts, we would end up well. Whenever something happens the thoughts that come up are automatic and most of the time these tend to be negative thoughts. However, a lot of us tend to go with the negative thoughts and our behavior ends up being negative as well. We go down a horrible path when we do not challenge the negative thoughts and choose a more positive and constructive way of looking at the situation.

There is also a possibility that we may not even go through the thought process stage but rather just move from an event to a behavior. Oftentimes, a lot of us deal with situations in that way. We do not think about what just happened; we move directly to showing what we feel (as demonstrated in our behavior). This is called impulsivity. Many times, a lot of us are impulsive and the result of impulsivity is rarely a positive outcome. Instead of going from event, thought process, to behavior, we go from the event to the behavior as shown below. We have to think about what we are thinking before we skip to behavior.

The following is a diagrammatic representation of this process.

Diagram C

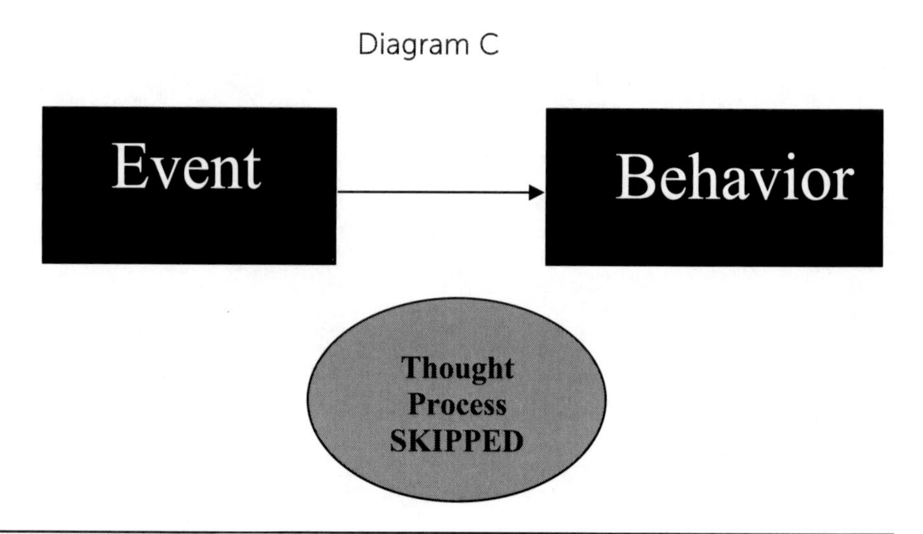

Note: **Thought Process** (This is where we challenge our thoughts and decide whether to follow the negative or positive train of thought)

Furthermore, if people realize that their thoughts are not going to produce positive results, they have a choice to "get rid" of those thoughts by beginning to think on the kinds of things that will produce the results they desire. We have to analyze the best thoughts that will produce the best outcomes. This is the stage where we become responsible for the resulting behaviors of our thought process.

What I have tried to do in the last several pages is lay the groundwork of the CBT treatment model and help us understand the power we have in changing the outcome of our thought processes. For most people, it is assumed that we have no control over what we think about. It may be true initially because our thoughts are largely automatic. This means that our thoughts usually follow what has just occurred, based on what is in our core beliefs, schema or "thought bank." If we have had many negative experiences or if we are used to hearing the adults around us (as we were growing up), express negative things about life, most likely our "thought bank" will be full of negative automatic thoughts. The opposite is also true. If we grew up around positive people or if we have had mostly positive experiences in life, then our "thought bank" will be full of positive thoughts. There are other issues that may lead us to having one kind of "thought bank" or the other but the environment we grew up in and our childhood experiences impact our thought patterns.

The good news, however, is that we do not have to be stuck with the "thought bank" we have always had. We can change. One of the major ways we can change our "thought bank," is by learning to pay attention to what we are thinking about. Paying attention to our thinking is an area a lot of individuals need to work on. If we do not work on monitoring our thought schema, we will continue to experience the same behaviors in situations because our thought process will be the same.

The purpose of this book is to use the thought monitoring, thought stopping and thought replacement process or the A-B-C model to show how someone who believes in the Bible can use certain scriptures to successfully stop their negative, non-productive thoughts by replacing them with what scripture says about their situation. To stop their negative thoughts and replace them with scripture, there are two presuppositions:

1. That the individual knows how to pay attention to their thought processes (thinking about what they are thinking about or thought monitoring) and to sort out those thoughts. They should know whether what they are thinking about is positive or something that will produce positive results and behaviors or not. In other words, they should be able to decipher

what they need to "keep" in their minds and what they need to discard. If they keep what should have been discarded, they should be ready to deal with the consequences of their choice in keeping with the train of that thought process.

2. The individual must know scripture. In addition, they need to know what scripture they need to use to defeat their negative thoughts and engage in a positive thought process. Of course, what scripture is used will depend on the issue at hand. Individuals cannot use scripture haphazardly and hope that it will produce positive results in their thought process. It is possible that such a situation could take place because of the power of God's word, but it would be better if individuals knew certain scriptural verses that pertain to their personal situations.

Furthermore, it is important to remember that it takes practice to become well versed in using thought monitoring, thought stopping and thought replacement (as we begin to delve into various situations and their corresponding scriptural references). Sometimes we get so used to responding via our automatic thoughts and other behaviors we have developed along the path of life that we do not realize that there is something wrong with the way we see things or the way we think about certain things. We believe that the way we respond to the situation is the way it should be responded to. However, God's word can show us some of our distorted ways of thinking. **We all have distorted thought patterns,** and there are several groups of those patterns. This topic on distorted thought patterns will be expounded on later in the text.

CHAPTER TWO

The Power of the Peace of God

Biblical Approach: Using Philippians 4:6-8.

As mentioned earlier, when I first learned about CBT while in graduate school, I immediately saw CBT as being based on Philippians 4:6-8.

"Do not be anxious about anything (*event/trigger*), but in every situation (*event/trigger*), by prayer and petition, with thanksgiving, present your requests to God (*thought replacement; instead of holding on to what is robbing me of my peace, I should pray, petition and give supplications*).

(7) And the peace of God which transcends all understanding, will guard your hearts and your minds in Christ Jesus (*the exchange that happens is that I realize that there is something robbing me of my peace (event/trigger)*.

These scriptures also delineate that if I tell God about my anxiety (*thought monitoring point*), He gives me peace in my heart and in mind (*thought replacement*) It is the lack of peace in my heart and my mind that causes me to become anxious or depressed or even afraid. If I continue to choose to be anxious or to allow thoughts that cause anxiety or depression to linger then my outward behavior will show through restlessness, trembling, sweating and other such symptoms. I may also feel my heart rate going up, nausea, dizziness, and fear of losing control. If I continue to allow feelings of anxiety or depression to rule my life, I would end up experiencing more serious forms of anxiety such as panic attacks, and at that point I may need to be medicated or even hospitalized in a psychiatric ward! Anxiety and depression, if managed early enough are two forms of mental illness that can be treated without requiring medication. Therapy may be needed to provide direction and interventions. Using the word of God to replace your fears with His peace can be one of the interventions, if used early enough and properly.

What the word of God is saying in the above verses can be represented in a diagram as follows:

Event Situation	Options	Results
Something happens that could lead me to being anxious, depressed, or afraid.	A) I can either choose to keep it to myself. OR B) I can choose to change my thoughts by telling God about it through praying, petitioning, and giving thanks when the event/trigger takes place.	A) Lead to anxiety, depression, fear, etc. OR B) He gives me His peace; He covers my mind and heart with peace through Jesus Christ.

Option B shows that we have exchanged something that could have possibly led to a full-blown anxiety or depressive episode without the peace of God. What this verse is telling us to do is what CBT teaches us. When something happens (event/antecedent/trigger), we can allow our automatic thoughts (which is what we start thinking about immediately something happens) to take over, resulting in any of the negative feelings which then lead to unwanted behaviors. By using scripture, we can replace our automatic thoughts with more positive thoughts. After we pray, petition, supplicate while giving thanks, concerning a trigger, we are afforded the peace of God. When we choose to do what we are instructed to do in Philippians 4:6-7, we are choosing to change the way we think about or see the event. Changing the way we think without a doubt, will change our behavior.

Peace is what is missing when we are experiencing anxiety, depression, or fear. Sometimes, it is because we feel we are not in control or we cannot control what is going on that causes us to lose our peace. In this case, coming to the realization that our heavenly Father is the source of peace is what we need to remember to bring our triggers to His immediate attention. Many times, we fear, become anxious or develop different negative behaviors because we do not know how things will end up. It is then that we really need to remember to stop our train of thought (thought stopping) and think about what is causing us to feel the way we are feeling. When we do so, we can think of a verse that addresses our issue and begin to think on that verse (replacing our negative thought), which would lead us to feeling at peace and our corresponding behaviors will match up with our thoughts.

One of the quickest verses for all of us to go to is 1 Peter 5:7. In the Amplified Bible (AMP) it reads: "casting all your cares [all your anxieties, all your worries, and all your concerns once and for all] on Him, for He cares about you [with deepest affection, and watches over you very carefully]." As we can see here, we are reminded or encouraged to cast (throw) all our cares (and the AMP Bible provides an extension of cares) upon Him. The word used is "casting" which is in the present continuous tense, meaning we should continuously cast our cares on Him. Every single time that we have a care, we must cast it upon Him. As implied by this verse, this is an on-going process. Casting our cares means that we have to do the work. When we discuss thought monitoring, thought stopping, and thought replacement we are not saying it's an easy process or a "one-time-fits-all process." However, like with everything else, the more we practice monitoring our thoughts and stopping the negative ones to replace them with positive ones, the easier the process will become for us.

There is a famous hymn *that states: "What a friend we have in Jesus,"* which goes on to say, *"...all our sins and griefs to bear, what a privilege to carry, everything to God in prayer. Oh, what peace we often forfeit, oh, what needless pain we bear, all because we do not carry everything to God in prayer."* According to this verse, we forfeit or lose our peace and we bear needless pain because we do not carry everything to God in prayer. The process of carrying everything to God is synonymous to replacing our negative thoughts. Whereas at first we were going to deal with whatever we are experiencing on our own, we now decide to carry it to God in prayer. For a Christian "carrying things" (thoughts and situations) that would cause distress, pain and so forth to God through prayer is one way of using thought monitoring. Thought monitoring for a Believer means challenging those anxious thoughts and replacing them by giving them to God in exchange for His peace. Peace is what we ultimately need as it replaces fear, anxiety, and depressive thoughts. We must learn to choose to let our Father know what our need is. If only we could learn how to cast those things (our cares) on Him, we would experience His peace. When we cast our cares on Him, we will not bear needless pain nor would we forfeit our peace. This is a truth and a promise to every child of God. The Lord Jesus left us with His peace. Jesus stated, "Peace I leave with you, my peace I give unto you...Let not your heart be troubled, neither let it be afraid" (John 14:27). He desires that we do not allow our hearts to be troubled but to live in His peace.

Therefore, whenever my heart begins to be troubled (by whatever reason or cause) I should quickly say, "Lord, You told me not to have my heart troubled because you left me peace; so now I cast this issue, that is causing me to be troubled, on you and I receive your peace." Remember, He already gave us His peace; therefore, we do not need to ask for it again. We just need to receive it or enter in that place of peace after we cast our cares on Him!

Maintaining the Peace

Learning how to use God's word to help us deal with various situations that would otherwise leave us feeling sad, scared, or depressed requires practice and belief that doing what the word says will produce the result it says it will. Going back to Philippians 4:6-7, we need to believe that if we let God know about our needs, He will hide our heart and mind in His peace which passes all understanding. What is even better is that in verse 8 of the same chapter, we are told what to do to maintain this peace, a great example of thought replacement. Apostle Paul states ".... whatever is true, whatever is honorable, whatever is just, whatever is pure, whatever is lovely, whatever is commendable, if there is any excellence, if there is anything worthy of praise, think about these things." (Phil 4:8, ESV). Isn't this amazing? Verse 8 clearly shows us that if we focus on what is true, honorable, just, pure, lovely, commendable and anything that is excellent and praiseworthy, we will not have to constantly deal with the negative feelings that lead us to anxiety, sadness, and depression. Again, for some, this process may happen quickly, but for others it may require repeated practice until we get to the point where our response is automatic.

To relate this to the CBT's thought monitoring and thought replacement model, individuals need to be aware of what they are thinking about. As soon as they realize what their thoughts are and if they do not measure up to any of the characteristics mentioned in Philippians 4:8, they need to "give" those thoughts to God according to Philippians 4:6. Obviously, this process calls for us to be involved in our thoughts. A lot of people do not realize that they have control over what they think about.

Thoughts have different sources and for the Christian, we usually say thoughts can be from you (automatic thoughts), they can be from the enemy, (negative, not life or joy giving), or they can be from the Lord (positive, righteous, peaceful, life giving and joyous). We always want our thoughts to be from the Lord; however, we were also given the ability to think, create etc. so there are thoughts that come from us. These thoughts may be positive or negative. It is an individual's job to monitor their thoughts or as Joyce Meyer would say to "think about what you are thinking about" (Meyer, 1995). Otherwise, we will follow the path of our thoughts. Just following our thoughts without asking ourselves if the thoughts will produce positive fruit for us, is what usually leads us to feelings that are negative and not productive.

There is a scripture in Proverbs 23 that states, "...as a man thinks in his heart so is he." We usually take this statement to mean if we think: "I will be rich" then, I will be rich. We can also think that whatever I think about is what I automatically become, which is erroneous. The verse, however, is helpful in our context because many times a person's outward actions can be deceiving, but a person's heart determines what a person is really like. What we think about determines what we are really like. We may show on the outside that we are hospitable people offering our guest food or drink, but if in our hearts we really don't want them to have it or not to eat it all, then we are not really the hospitable person we are portraying. Instead we are a begrudging person that wants to create this generous picture. In the same way, if we carry feelings of depression, anxiety, fear or whatever else, we may try hard to portray that we are happy or not scared so people can think we are good Christians, but the question becomes, what is in our hearts? What are we feeling, or thinking? As an individual, it is my job to ensure that what I am really thinking is explored and brought into view and if it does not align with Philippians 4:8 for example, then I have work to do on the heart level.

It is interesting that in the Bible thoughts are mentioned in relation to the heart ("As a man thinks in his heart..., ``"Let not your heart be troubled..." (John 14;1), whereas in psychology they are mentioned with regards to the mind. It seems in the Bible, the mind and heart are one and the same, as far as the issue of thoughts and decision making is concerned. As such, our responsibility as a child of God is to monitor what is in our minds and hearts, "... for out of the abundance of the heart, the mouth speaks" (Matthew 12:34, ESV). It may be better to ask God to help us understand the connection between our minds and hearts so that we can be vigilant to cast their contents on Him. Being vigilant about our thoughts will ensure that our outward and inward parts align, that is, our thoughts will line up with our actions.

CHAPTER THREE

The Power of Patience

CBT Approach: Thought Monitoring (Thinking About What One is Thinking About)

In this chapter we will get into the nitty gritty of how one can apply CBT tools to God's word to change the outcome of their negative/undesirable thoughts. We will do so by looking at the following subtopics:

- Thought Monitoring (thinking about what one is thinking about):

The process of learning how to monitor or pay attention to our thoughts can be tedious and long, but like with everything worth doing, the results can be life changing. When we master monitoring our thoughts, it becomes second nature to us, and it helps us from making impulsive decisions. Not mastering thought monitoring is a sure way that we will keep making decisions impulsively or we will keep reacting to situations. If you go back to the CBT basic model of event >>>>>> thought monitoring>>>>>>>behavior or to the, A-B-C model of antecedent/trigger>>>>>>>behaviors/beliefs>>>>>>consequence s, it appears as if there is always this neat pattern in which things happen. However, it is not always like this. Many times, most of us do not take the time to think about what just happened (the event or antecedent), we just react to it. We skip a whole step in the middle. The step that is skipped is thought monitoring, thinking about what we are thinking about or better yet, thinking about what just happened. When we do not take the time to review our thoughts, to explore how we are thinking about what just happened to us, we are likely going to react to the situation impulsively.

One of the major negative behaviors that thought-stopping should counteract is impulsivity. Impulsivity happens because we do not stop to think about the outcome of our responses to an event. Instead, we allow ourselves to go from an event happening to showing our behavior or from an antecedent to consequences of our reaction. Many times, decisions or reactions made from impulsivity are not good decisions and are regrettable, whereas monitoring our thoughts gives us the opportunity to decide how we want to respond to the situation.

Reacting to a situation is an immediate response to a situation and is defined by the Merriam-Webster as "...the act or process or an *instance of reacting*".

Decisions made in an instance of reacting will cause us to end up in trouble. We should learn to follow the entire process of being faced with an event, thinking about that event then choosing how to respond to it. The word, "respond" includes a component of thinking about something, reviewing it, then deciding on a course of action, whereas "react" implies impulsivity.

As Christians, one of the virtues we are encouraged to develop is patience. Patience is also a part of the fruit of the Spirit mentioned in Galatians 5:22. If we know that as a child of God we lack patience, we need to make the time to memorize and recite Galatians 5:22. Being patient rewards us in many ways including during the important process of monitoring our thoughts (thinking about what we are thinking about) and challenging what does not line up with the will of God for us.

For example, if I am someone who has not developed the virtue of patience and something happens, I will quickly exhibit the behavior of my reaction to the situation, reached impulsively, based on my automatic thoughts. I will not have stopped at the thought-monitoring stage to process what I am thinking about with regards to the situation and why. The result of not processing the thought will be a poor decision whose consequence I have to deal with, possibly resulting in depression, fear or anxiety.

One other scripture that would help us to think about our responses (when we monitor our thoughts) as opposed to our reactions is Proverbs 3:5-6 "... trust in the Lord with all your heart...

There is a place for impulsive or instantaneous decisions; decisions driven by our intuition such as when an object falls in the fire, we quickly scoop it out. Another example of a positive impulsive decision is if a child hits themselves against an object, we quickly pick them up to comfort them. Those are some of the many specific situations that our bodies are wired to respond to by reacting to prevent harm or injury; however, other situations should be given the right amount of thought and time before choosing a course of action.

Trust His Voice

The process of thought monitoring for a child of God includes the ability to trust in God and to wait until He reveals the way one should go. In Proverbs 3:5-6, we are admonished to, "Trust in the Lord with all your heart; and lean not unto your own understanding. But in all thy ways acknowledge him, and he shall direct your paths." The above verse is urging us as children of God to trust and rely on Him. We are reminded not to lean on our own understanding but to trust as we wait. When we make impulsive decisions and simply react to a situation, we are failing to follow these instructions which come with a reward. The reward is having our paths being directed by God. For us to have our paths directed by God, we must be able to wait on Him during a time of decision making.

In addition, trusting His ways involves listening in to what God is saying to us through His Holy Spirit. In Isaiah 30:21, we are reminded that our ears shall hear a word behind us, saying, "this is the way, walk in it, when you turn to the right or when you turn to the left." One of the assumptions of this verse is that we take the time to listen to our "Teacher" so we can know where He is leading us. God knows the affliction that we may face, but He is faithful to walk us through the right path that we should take.

Part of monitoring our thoughts involves seeking God and waiting to hear from His Spirit. He has a path set for us and therefore He will redirect us whenever we veer to the right or the left. We can know the path he has set for us during the process of monitoring our thoughts when we choose to wait for His direction. Part of our responsibility as children of God is to develop the habit of waiting on God. When we develop this ability, it will become easier for us to be patient as we wait for His direction. Decision making for a child of God involves waiting on Him. The act of waiting does not mean we will not be doing anything in the meantime. When we wait there is action that must be taking place, and for us that action should include actively listening into what the Lord is or could be saying to us. Decisions made hastily without clear direction from the Lord will usually lead to negative outcomes. However, for decisions that need to be made quickly, if we govern ourselves according to the guidance of the Holy Spirit, we will be able to make the right decision as we monitor our thoughts under His guidance. Some ways that we can assess if our decisions are right is if we feel peace and joy about a decision.

Analyzing the Event (Trigger/Situation)

The process of thought monitoring should help us in identifying the event that has led us to be where we are in our thought process. In other words, we would not be in a place of thinking about our options or waiting on the Lord to direct us if nothing had happened. It is important to think about the event and challenge our thoughts arising from that event. When we take the time to think about the event, we may find out that we do not need to behave or feel (sadness, fear, anxiety) in that moment.

The above-mentioned stage also enables us to learn how to be patient and true with ourselves. Thinking about what took place (event/situation/antecedent) and realizing that this is how we usually respond or react to similar situations should help us know that we may have a distorted (negative) way of looking at certain issues. Distorted thinking patterns also known as cognitive distortions are, "exaggerated or irrational thought patterns involved in the onset or perpetuation of psychopathological states such as depression and anxiety.... Cognitive distortions are thoughts that cause individuals to perceive reality inaccurately. (Beck, 1976). Beck further explains that when reality is perceived inaccurately, it leads to the beginning or continuation of mental health issues such as anxiety and depression. Therefore, it is important for us to challenge our thought process so we can see if we are perceiving the issue at hand (event) properly. As Christians, one way we use to challenge the onset of these mental health issues is the word of God.

In addition, Dr. Beck goes on to explain in his cognitive model, that looking at reality negatively, "is a factor in symptoms of emotional dysfunction and poorer subjective well-being. Specifically, negative thinking patterns reinforce negative emotions and thoughts. (Beck, 1976). If we always think about issues negatively, we will most likely end up feeling depressed or anxious, according to this theory. Therefore, as Christians we need God's word to help us challenge our thoughts, especially if they usually tend to be mostly negative thoughts.

One can encourage oneself by reciting Isaiah 55:8-9:

8"For my thoughts are not your thoughts,
Neither are your ways my ways, declares the Lord.
9 For as the heavens are higher than the earth,
so are my ways higher than your ways
and my thoughts than your thoughts. (NKJV)

Meditating on the words above can encourage people to start looking at their situation positively even if it may be a negative situation. It is comforting to know that God's way of looking at our situations is much higher than we may ever look at the same situation. It is important to include the Lord in how we see or think about various situations. For a child of God, part of our thought monitoring and thought replacing process is to include what God's word says about the situation. Continue to read the Bible and memorize God's word because the Holy Spirit will bring to the surface what you have hidden in your heart.

There is an advantage to hiding God's word in our hearts. It helps us not to sin. We usually think of sin as something we do or commit that is against God's word or that does not line up with His word. However, not submitting our thoughts to God or not thinking in line with God's word can be considered as sin. Making a decision without applying God's word (from what is hidden in our hearts) could lead us to sin or we could be leaning on our own understanding instead of allowing the Lord to direct our paths. In the language of Cognitive Behavioral Therapy, we must monitor our thoughts, challenge the current thoughts with God's word and replace negative thoughts with positive ones (or God's word) which will lead us into making proper decisions. These proper decisions mean that we will not sin against Him.

Remember, Philippians 4:6-7 tells us to not be anxious about anything but instead by following specific steps (telling God about our need or situation, praying, thanksgiving and making supplications or petitioning) which leads our hearts and minds to be covered by the peace of God which passes all understanding. We are further reminded in 1 Peter 5:7-9 ...casting all your anxieties on him, because he cares for you." (ESV) or "casting all your cares upon Him; for he cares for you" NKJV) This is another instance in the Bible that reminds us that we are not meant to carry our own anxieties, cares, worries and concerns. No wonder we get stressed out, depressed and anxious or fearful when we do!

CHAPTER FOUR

The Power of Pushing Out Fear

Biblical Approach: Using Scripture to Remove Fear

Like most things, paranoia or fear can be looked at from a spiritual point of view as well as a psychological perspective. In one of Apostle Joshua Selman's messages, he states that fear is a spirit that opens the door to other attacks on our lives. (Joshua Selman, Christ Gospel Church, Nigeria). If undealt with, fear can lead to other issues settling in our lives such as the inability to do anything or move forward because we are paralyzed by it. In addition, undealt with fear holds us back from walking into our destiny. Whether thinking about fear from a spiritual or psychological perspective, it is an emotion that needs to be dealt with because of the negative consequences it brings in our lives.

Fear is an emotion that we all have felt at one time or another and there are many different causes of fear. In the article, "Helping Children and Adolescents Cope with Violence and Disasters" found in Relias Learning.com, it is stated that, "Fear is perhaps the most common response to trauma." Fear is a common response that does not only affect children but adults as well. It is important to remember that there are some issues, fear being one of them, which happen to individuals in their childhood but never gets resolved as they grow up. Therefore, there may be many adults carrying around fear (and other emotions) that were caused by various traumatic situations in their childhood but never got dealt with. It is not only children and adolescents we have to worry about as clinicians. There are some fears in adults that must be explored to identify their source and when they may have started, so that they can be treated.

To show the prevalence of fear and the importance of dealing with it, the Bible addresses the issue in several verses such as Isaiah 41:10:

"Fear not, for I am with you;
Be not dismayed, for I am your God.
I will strengthen you,
Yes, I will help you,
I will uphold you with My righteous right hand." (NKJV).

God was encouraging Jacob (the children of Israel in this case) not to fear based on what they were faced with at the time. God assures Jacob of what He will do to help him (Jacob) in his time of need (when faced with fear). It is important to remember that as Christians, every word, every promise, every correction and whatever else that is in the Bible is applicable to us. So, what the Lord was saying to Jacob in the above verses, can be applicable to our lives. We can insert our name where it says Jacob and seek the assurance that the Lord was offering to Jacob. As you continue to read the quoted chapter you see in verses 14 and 15 how the Lord comforts and encourages the men of Israel not to fear. It is interesting that He refers to them as, "O worm Jacob!" A worm is spineless; it is almost without protection. When we allow fear to rule over our lives, we become like worms. We become like people with no strength and no protection. Fear zaps us of all the strength and courage that we may once have had! However, the Lord reminds Jacob in his worm-like state to:

"Fear not, you worm Jacob, you men of Israel! I am the one who helps you, declares the LORD; your Redeemer is the Holy One of Israel" (Isaiah 41:14).

As Christians, we need to memorize this verse so that when we are fearful, we can ask ourselves: What is causing me to be fearful? Is the event, (trigger, antecedent) that is making me fearful real or is it not (this is the process of thought monitoring once something has occurred). At this point we should either say, "This is not real; I am just fearful or yes, the event is real and it's okay that I am feeling this way, but this is what the word of God tells me to do when I am fearful." After you observe a train of thought, you go on to recite the verses about what God says about fear. We ***repeat the verses continuously*** until the fear subsides. Alongside repeating the verse, we need to develop a deep understanding and belief of who God says He is. He declares in the above verses that He is our helper, that He is our Redeemer, that He is the one who upholds or takes care of us. In verse 15 He declares what He will make us to become if we trust in Him: "*...a threshing sledge, new and sharp, with many teeth...*" God is able to turn us into fierce individuals if we allow ourselves to trust Him. We continue to repeat the Word of God until it is immersed in our hearts. We repeat the Word of God until we believe it and until we become one with it. It is this level of belief that helps to change our old way of looking at things. It helps us to develop a new mindset and gets rid of our unhealthy thinking patterns, in this case, fear.

There are some mindsets that can be seen as strongholds. Having a stronghold means that this mindset has such a grip on us that we cannot easily shake it off. It takes continued repetition of the appropriate verses from the Bible to bring certain mindsets down. Most of us know these words, "For the weapons of our warfare are not carnal but mighty in God...". A lot of us stop right there, but these words are part of a particularly powerful set of verses that are helpful in dealing with strongholds. The set of verses I am referring to are found in

2 Corinthians 10:3-5:

"3 For though we walk in the flesh, we do not war according to the flesh. 4 For the weapons of our warfare are not carnal but mighty in God for pulling down strongholds, 5 casting down arguments and every high thing that exalts itself against the knowledge of God, bringing every thought into captivity to the obedience of Christ," (NKJV).

OR

"3 For though we walk in the flesh, we are not waging war according to the flesh. 4 For the weapons of our warfare are not of the flesh but have divine power to destroy strongholds. 5 We destroy arguments and every lofty opinion raised against the knowledge of God, and take every thought captive to obey Christ" (ESV).

Spiritual Weapons to Combat Fear

The weapons of prayer, faith, declarations, etc. are mighty in God for the pulling down of strongholds (also called fortresses or negative thinking patterns) from our minds and emotions. In CBT, we use anxiety management techniques such as deep muscle relaxation and deep breathing to help individuals get relief from their stressors. However, as a Christian we use these techniques alongside the Word of God.

We combat fear through saying a declaration. We can declare, "I am not afraid or fearful, and quote or declare verse 4 and 5, particularly repeating verse 5 and mentioning, "My weapons are mighty in God for pulling down strongholds, I am casting down arguments and I cast down every high thing, I cast down fear, anxiety, depression that wants to exalt itself against the knowledge of God in my life; anything that raises itself above the knowledge of God and I take every thought captive to obey Christ." You can create your own declarations that specifically deal with your fear.

Another way to combat fears is to constantly be filled with the things of God. This means reciting verses, singing, and making melody in our heart to the Lord according to Ephesians 5:19-20. Singing has a way of lifting our spirits. Think of a song. It can be a hymn, a worship song, or whatever exalts God, and watch how your attitude changes! Another way of filling your heart with the things of God is by reciting or remembering what Philippians 4:8 says, ".... whatever is true, whatever is honorable, whatever is just, whatever is pure, whatever is lovely, 1whatever is commendable, if there is any excellence, if there is anything worthy of praise, think about these things" (ESV). Part of our success after we have thought on noble things is that now we have to, "...destroy arguments and every lofty opinion raised against the knowledge of God and take every thought captive to obey Christ." We must replace or fill the space vacated by the lofty opinions that were raised against God with what God's Word says about that situation. Our thought process was consumed by these lofty opinions and thoughts that were against the knowledge of Christ or they consumed us instead of us being consumed by the thoughts of God.

When we focus on depressive thoughts, thoughts that arouse anxiety or fear, or any other thoughts that do not align with acknowledging God or focusing on Him, we usually end up experiencing some mental health symptoms (depression, anxiety, or fear). It is proven that milder forms of depression are caused when we focus inwardly on our situations instead of looking outwardly to find hope for our situations. Focusing on God is looking outwardly. Focusing on our situations and wondering how we will resolve the issues at hand or feeling sorry for ourselves is carrying opinions and thoughts that are against Christ. We have to know how to deploy the godly strategies given to us to combat fear before it opens up doors to many other things. God has given us strategies that are powerful and effective. We can use the CBT method to challenge our thoughts that do not line up with God's word and then replace those irrational thoughts with what the word of God says.

One more verse to help us when dealing with fear (in other words, recite and believe this verse to replace feelings of fear) is found in Psalm 56:3-4:

> 3 Whenever I am afraid,
> I will trust in You.
> 4 In God (I will praise His word),
> In God I have put my trust.
> I will not fear.
> What can flesh do to me?

I particularly like verse 3, "Whenever I am afraid, I will trust in You." How many of us can say that we turn our trust to the Lord when we are afraid? David did. The Psalm was written when he was captured by his enemy, the Philistines. I believe this was a vicious army, and I am not sure whether David had hope of being alive after he was captured. However, during his time of intense fear, he was able to declare that he would still trust in God! What a testimony of David's deep trust in the Lord. Many of us, whenever we are faced with a tough or fearful situation, instead of drawing closer to God, we pull away from Him. We sometimes also get mad at Him for allowing us to be in the situation. It is at such times that we need to monitor how we are thinking about the situation and God. If we sense fear, instead of drawing away from God, we should replace the thoughts of fear by declaring, like David did, "Whenever I am afraid, I will trust in You...In God I have put my trust, I will not fear. What can flesh do to me?" Notice that David said, "what can flesh do to me?" because he was being pursued by a man. You can replace the word, 'flesh' with whatever is causing you to be afraid. A sure way of defeating fear is knowing what His word says about fear. It is important to understand that God knew fear would paralyze us and would open doors to other spirits or irrational thoughts.

Paul states that, "For God has not given us the spirit of fear, but of power and of love and of a sound mind" (2 Timothy 1:7). Instead of giving us the spirit of fear (or a spirit of fear according to other translations) God gave us three distinct spirits. We can extend the second part of the verse as follows, "but He has given us the spirit of power and the spirit of love and the spirit of a sound mind" as shown by the use of "and" between power, love, and a sound mind. So, when we are fearful or afraid, we can conclude that we are not operating in power, we are not operating in love (perfect love casts out all fear according to 1 John 4:8) and we are not operating with a sound mind (a stable mind that is able to make good judgement). The moment we realize we are beginning to feel fearful; we should begin to declare that we have not been given a spirit of fear. After that, you call on the spirit the Lord says we have been given. We have been given a spirit of power, love, and a sound mind. Declaring what spirit He has given us will help us to overcome fear thereby closing any doors it may have opened in our lives. We will also be able to walk in power, in love and in sound judgement, discipline and self-control (a sound mind). As we practice these things we will begin to see that we are overcoming things that used to hold us down before!

CHAPTER FIVE

The Power of Planting His Word

CBT and Biblical Approach: Challenge Negative Automatic Thoughts (unhealthy thoughts that come up immediately after an event happens and replace them with God's Word).

As mentioned earlier, automatic thoughts can be positive or negative, although the term is usually taken to have a negative connotation. Negative automatic thoughts stem from cognitive distortions. According to the Merriam-Webster dictionary, a distortion is "...the act of twisting or altering something out of its true, natural or original state." Cognitive (or thought) distortions are not representative of the truth because they are altered or twisted truth. Cognitive distortions are also referred to as faulty thinking patterns or faulty mindsets. It is a problem if we act based on our distortions because we are not acting based on the truth. Therefore, distortions need to be identified, challenged, and discarded. They are distortions because they cause individuals to perceive reality inaccurately (Beck, 1976). Perceiving reality inaccurately (or based on faulty thinking patterns) leads to believing things that are not true and if those beliefs are not challenged one may end up feeling depressed, anxious, discouraged, fearful, etc. It is important that we learn how to "review" our thoughts before acting on them. When we find out that our automatic thoughts are negative or not based on reality, it is our job to replace them with positive thoughts or thoughts that are based on reality. For the Christian, our reality is the Word of God.

Common Cognitive Distortions:

Having looked at some common scriptures and how to use them in dealing with our faulty thinking patterns and negative core beliefs, in the following sections let us look at some common cognitive distortions or faulty thinking patterns. Remember that cognitive distortions are common, entirely normal, and not our fault but when unhelpful thinking styles are present in our lives to an excessive degree they are associated with poor mental health (Psychology Tools). It is important that we look at some of the common cognitive distortions (negative core beliefs) so we can know, or at least begin to deal with them when we realize they are a part of our schema.

10 Common Cognitive Distortions

1. **Mind Reading**: Mind reading is when people assume that they know what someone is thinking while not having sufficient proof of what the person is really thinking about. Mind reading can happen when we base a decision of what we think someone is thinking about on an act. For example, one can think, "She does not think I am good at anything" based on how the person may have concluded that they were "looked at" after they did something that was not a success. A good example may be if a group of people are playing a game together and the person in question has a turn, but they do not do as well and immediately one person on their team looks at another. The person whose turn it was to play but did

not do so well may conclude erroneously, that the two were looking at each other to communicate how poor she is at the game.

2. **Fortune Telling:** This is when an individual predicts the future that things will get worse than they are presently or that there is danger ahead but without specific evidence. For example, "I know I will not be hired for the position." This is a distorted way of looking at things because people can be stopped or can stop themselves from pursuing their dreams because they are already "fortune telling or foretelling" an outcome of something without any evidence of their belief. This distortion is also known as **jumping to conclusions**. If you realize that you tend to be a fortune teller, work on restructuring this mindset with the appropriate scriptures such as Proverbs 3:5-6. This way you can begin to trust God as you move forward in your decision-making process.
3. **Catastrophizing**: Have you ever found yourself believing that something is going to go wrong but when it happens it is not as bad as you feared? If you have, you were engaged in catastrophizing. In catastrophizing, our reality is based on our distortion that things are always awful or terrible for us. We have allowed a mindset to settle in us that believes things never work out for us; as a result, we assume that whatever else will happen is going to follow the same pattern. It is unlike God's nature to allow us to face failures in our lives forever. There may be a season in our lives when things do not seem to work out, and usually God allows those seasons so we can learn to trust Him and to grow from those experiences. However, it is never God's nature to allow us to live in a state of permanent defeat. Catastrophizing is believing that things will be awful and unbearable for us,

without specific proof of our fear. For example one can say: "It would be awful if they left me. I would never make it without them." As God's children, we should always trust that God is taking care of us and that He will work things out for us especially when we cannot figure it out. A good scripture to remember if you engage in catastrophizing is Romans 8:28, "And we know that for those who love God all things work together for good, for those who are called according to his purpose" (ESV). The key here is that you love God and that you know that you are called according to his purpose.

4. **Labelling**: This is when an individual assigns a generalization to or generalizes negative traits either to oneself or to others, usually without any evidence of the statement being made. For example, "No one likes me," Or saying, "They are always talking about me." Such statements are usually not based on the truth but on one's assumptions stemming from a distorted mindset or false core beliefs about self and others. If we tend to label ourselves, we can change this mindset by using what the Word of God says about us. If one knows what God says about them, it becomes irrelevant what others think or say about them. One can also help themselves by asking others how they are thought of.
5. **Negative Filter**: Have you ever come across someone who usually never seems to say anything positive or good about themselves? If so, this person may be someone that has a negative filter. Negative filtering is when an individual usually focuses mainly or exclusively on the negatives in his or her life but rarely notices the positive. For example he or she may say, "Look at all these mistakes I always make." The reality may be that they may have made one or a couple mistakes. Usually

in negative filtering the person does not take into consideration all the other times they have done something correctly. This is a mindset that, like most core beliefs, may have come out of being criticized or being told that they never did anything right. As an individual, one needs to work on finding a new identity based on what the Lord says about him, so he can begin to believe that there are some things that he does well and that not everything he does is a mistake or is wrong. Realizing and believing that God made us special (Psalm 139:14) is helpful in changing this mindset.

6. **Overgeneralizing**: This happens when we develop a pattern of negatives based on a single incident. In other words, we overgeneralize when we draw a conclusion about our ability or other's abilities based on an individual occurrence of something. For example one may think, "This generally happens to me; I seem to mess up all the time." The reality could be this may be the first time this kind of mistake has happened. Believing in overgeneralized statements like the one above eventually leads us to a place where we may become totally blind to any positive incidents. It is important for a child of God to remember to refrain from statements that negate God's word regarding His creation. We are "wonderfully and fearfully made..." (Psalm 139:14) is what the word of God says about us. How can something wonderful and fearful always make mistakes?
7. **Shoulds**: When we use shoulds, we allow events to be interpreted in terms of how things ***should*** be in the future instead of focusing on what is here now. For example, one may say, "I should pass this exam. If I don't, then I am a failure." In this case, I am already labelling myself based on an outcome that is not even

here yet. Shoulds usually appear as rules we set for ourselves or others and if those rules are not met, we feel like failures. Must and ought stem from the same mindset as shoulds. Sometimes should is used to "cry over spilt milk", as in "I should have known he couldn't be trusted." In this case we are implying that there are negative consequences we are dealing with now because we did not know the individual's character trait of untrustworthiness. Some of us may have been told not to focus on "shoulda, woulda, coulda" because when we do so, we take our focus from the present and the future but concentrate on the past. Focusing on the past does not change anything except rob us of the precious mental and emotional effort we should be exerting on our current and future situations.

8. Magnification and minimization: This is when one tends to magnify what is negative and minimize what is positive in one's life. In magnification an individual tends to place more emphasis on insignificant events at the expense of what is significant. So, people may focus on a mistake they made and continue to talk about that while more important issues such as personal achievements are minimized or lessened or even altogether ignored. People who function out of the magnification and minimization cognitive distortion mindset typically blow their problem out of proportion or exaggerate its impact. On the other hand, they minimize or fail to focus on the positive aspects of their life. It is as if they choose not to or are unable to see the positives in their lives but are likely to talk about the negative aspects of their lives. An example of magnification and minimization would be if one were asked to give a speech for an occasion. He may do very well giving the speech even

though he may have made a couple of minor slip ups; however, after the speech he may find it hard to receive the compliments given to him for a moving speech because his focus is on the errors he made. Such a person would completely miss out on the fun or importance of their contribution because he put much emphasis on the small mistakes he made. When we tend to magnify the minor events in life and not recognize the important things or the truth about the events, we set ourselves up for anxiety or panic attacks. Thinking about a negative incident repeatedly tends to provoke anxiety. For people who tend to have this distortion, Philippians 4:6-8 and any other verse that speaks to not being anxious are important verses to memorize. Let us not allow our small mishaps to crowd our thinking to the point that we fail to see the many good things that we are achieving.

9. Blaming: People who engage in this cognitive distortion hold others responsible for their own emotional pain. They may be heard saying statements like: "Don't make me feel bad about what I am doing." They forget that no one can make anyone else feel pain or shame, or whatever emotion; We are the only ones that have control over our emotions and reactions. People who engage in blaming may even blame themselves for every problem they face, even those out of their control. Individuals may engage in this cognitive distortion because they may have been blamed for their mistakes as children and as a result, they internalized blame. These individuals will need to trust that God loves them and does not focus on their mistakes but on their strengths. These individuals will have to learn what Romans 8:1 states: "There is now therefore no

condemnation to them which are in Christ Jesus, who walk not after the flesh, but after the Spirit." They will need to understand that just as God does not condemn them, they should not condemn themselves nor allow anyone else to condemn them or feel condemned by anyone.

10. Polarized Thinking or Black and White Thinking: This is the distorted thinking pattern that makes us believe that we must be perfect or else we are a complete failure. In this distortion, there are no gray areas. Everything to us is either black or white and right or wrong. This cognitive distortion is also known as the "all or nothing" thinking distortion. People with polarized thinking always think of people or things in either or categories. As individuals, we need to learn to give others and situations grace and believe that there is a possibility that something can be in the gray zone.

It is important to remember that we all have some type of distorted way of looking at life. Knowing some of those distortions helps us in deciding how to deal with them so that we can look at reality in a realistic manner. Also, remember that our distortions do not speak to who God says we are, they are based on past experiences which may have been true or not. As we grow in the Lord, we should be able to identify some of our distortions based on his Word so that we may begin to replace them with the correct way God sees us and how we should see ourselves.

It is through the process of reviewing what we are thinking about and examining if it is based on reality or not that we have a chance to change the outcome of our thoughts. If our thoughts are not reality based (but based on emotions or our automatic thoughts, and therefore distorted), we should challenge them and seek to replace them with thoughts that are reality based (that are true, honorable, just, pure, lovely, and so forth according to Philippians 4:8). It is at this point that we can change the outcome of our thought process. For a child of God, it is not enough just to have positive feel-good statements; it is imperative that some of those auspicious statements are based on God's word and that they are used to uproot all the distortions we have believed based on our past experiences. Scripture reminds us that:

> *For the word of God is living and active, sharper than any two-edged sword, piercing to the division of soul and of spirit, of joints and of marrow, and discerning the thoughts and intentions of the heart. And no creature is hidden from his sight, but all are naked and exposed to the eyes of him to whom we must give account (Hebrews 4:12-16, ESV).*

For a child of God, His word can ***pierce and divide*** (separate or expose) the contents of our souls (our humanly realm; mind, emotions and will power) from the spirit (the spirit of God that He breathed in us and is a part of us and connects us to him on a deeper level than our thoughts or feelings). God's word is also able to **divide** joints from the marrow. It can ***discern*** (judge or know) the thoughts and intentions of the heart. God's word has the power and ability **to judge** (know) our thoughts and the plans of our heart. Because it can do that (discern); surely His word can help us know if our automatic thoughts are positive or negative. His Word can help us figure out what our negative automatic thoughts are based on. He can bring to our remembrance the events or activities that took place for us to develop those negative cognitive distortions. By reading and studying His Word, with the help of the

Holy Spirit, we will begin to discover passages and verses that will help in challenging our negative distortions.

Challenging negative thoughts and replacing them with scriptures will help us to have a "bank" of positive automatic thoughts. The new bank of positive automatic thoughts will be based on God's word and what it says about us. We want our automatic thoughts to be positive and life giving. We want our mindset to be based on the life-giving Word of God. As we recite and come to believe what the Word of God says about us and the various experiences we will go through, it can change the contents of our mind. According to Jeremiah 1:10, His Word will "...uproot out and pull down" everything that does not line up with His will for our life. Making the declarations will, "...destroy and throw down" anything and everything that has come to destroy the plans that He has for our life. When we speak His Word over our lives it will, "...build and plant" in us the plans He had for us when He formed us in our mother's womb (Jeremiah 1:10).

CHAPTER SIX

The Power of Acknowledging our Feelings

CBT Approach: Identifying Feelings and Resulting Behaviors Following our Thought Process

Another important step in CBT is identifying feelings and resulting behaviors following our thought process. Once we have examined our thoughts and understood their trigger, it is important that we identify how we are feeling. Failure to stop at this process could be what ends us up into depression, anxiety, or fear. According to CBT, our thoughts lead to how we feel and our feelings lead to our behaviors. If I am feeling positive about something that recently occurred, then my outward behavior will reflect those feelings. In the same way, if a trigger or event causes me to automatically think negatively, then my behavior is going to reflect my thoughts. Occasional negative thoughts are not an issue. Even though cognitive distortions are normal, it becomes damaging when our thinking styles **are excessively distorted**. Excessive distortions lead to the likelihood of people dealing with poor mental health. Constantly thinking negatively can take the form of, "Poor me; nothing good ever happens to me" or "I will never amount to anything" and so forth. Watch these kinds of thoughts because the feelings that come out of them are not helpful for us and do not line up with God's will for us.

The process of getting rid of negative automatic thoughts or cognitions is the practical and perhaps most difficult part of changing our way of thinking and therefore, the feelings that follow. The Dictionary of Psychology describes automatic thoughts in two ways as:

1. "Thoughts that are instantaneous, habitual and non-conscious. Automatic thoughts affect mood and actions."
2. "Thoughts that have been so well learned and habitually repeated that they occur without cognitive effort."

These are the automatic thoughts that we do not have to think about. They are negative automatic thoughts; they simply pop up. These are probably thoughts that lead to behaviors that when we see them in people we think, "How could he think that way?" or "What was he thinking?" We referred to these types of thoughts as strongholds when we talked about 2 Corinthians 10:3-5. We could also say this is how we are hard wired or programmed so that if anything happens, we automatically have a way we think about it. To change and reduce the occurrence of most mental health issues (which are really behaviors coming out of our poor or negative thinking processes), we must undo the hard wiring in our minds or hearts. We need to begin to feed ourselves with what the Word of God says so that with practice we can be able to respond differently next time a similar issue happens.

We monitor our thoughts to ensure that we do not have an excess amount of negative thoughts. Decreasing the existence of negative thoughts helps us to prevent an influx of negative feelings and therefore negative behaviors. For a Christian, once we discover a presence of negative thoughts in our life, we want to find scripture that addresses the nature of our negative thoughts. It is perfectly fine for a child of God to use the conventional tools of dealing with cognitive distortions, but alongside those, use the word of God because of the power it possesses to "discern the thoughts and intentions of the heart."

New Patterns After Thought Replacement

After identifying negative thoughts and replacing them with positive thoughts, observe the new thought patterns following thought replacement.

Again, it is important to understand that we want to aim at totally changing the way we see things and start seeing them based on what God's word says. ***Our goal should be to get to a place where our automatic thoughts evoke God's word when something happens to us. God's word should not be an afterthought, it should be what comes to our minds immediately when something happens.*** God's word is what will eventually change our core beliefs. Core beliefs are the center of our automatic thoughts. Whatever we believe about something (core belief) is what we will immediately think about when something in that arena happens. Cognitive behavioral therapy teaches us that the only way we can prevent this from happening is by changing our core beliefs. We change our core beliefs according to what God's word says.

Core beliefs create the automatic thoughts we have when something occurs. As stated earlier, our core beliefs are usually due to something that may have happened to us in our childhood and they determine how we view the world around us. Core beliefs can be both positive and negative. It is the negative ones that cause concern. CBT teaches that to change our negative core beliefs we must go through cognitive restructuring

Identify Distorted Thought Patterns

The Word of God is a great tool to help us realize where our thoughts are distorted or where they do not line up with what His word says. For a child of God, anything (thought, action, emotion) that does not agree or line up with the Word of God is a distorted thought pattern. The Word of God is our yardstick or plumbline. The way we think, act and feel should line up with how the Bible instructs us. We need our faith to grow because that is the only way we will be liberated from "seeing" things the way we have always seen them and start seeing them according to how God sees them. Jesus mentions in Matthew 6:33 that we must seek the Kingdom of God first. By telling us to seek the Kingdom of God first, the Lord is telling us to change our focus. As Believers, we have to focus on the Kingdom of God and the things that seem so important to us will not seem as important. That is cognitive restructuring; we change the way we used to look at the cares of this world by focusing on God's Kingdom and gaining an understanding that our Heavenly Father knows that we have a need for basic necessities, for example. Yes, basic necessities like food and clothing may still be important but not in the same way they used to be before.

In Luke 12:22-34, in a section titled "Do Not Worry", the Lord goes to great lengths in reminding us the importance of seeking His kingdom first (vs.31). In vs. 25 He asks, "And which of you by worrying can add one cubit to his stature?" In other words, who can lengthen their life by the distance between the elbow and the tip of the middle finger by worrying? Worrying, fretting, and negative thoughts do not add anything to our lives. As mentioned earlier, engaging in such thought patterns could take away from our life because we end up developing anxiety and other mental health issues. We have all probably heard that worrying causes ulcers and other health issues such as high blood pressure. The Lord knew about this and He warned us against worrying, rather he encouraged us to remember that we are more important to our Father who takes care of creation that is not as important (sparrows), and He also keeps count of our hair. To develop this level of faith or core belief, we must get rid of whatever we believed before and press on God (could be by repeating the verse over and over) until we can get to a level of faith that helps us to trust and believe what His word says to us.

CHAPTER SEVEN

The Power of Applying His Promises

Biblical Approach: Scriptures to Memorize and Repeat

The following are examples on how to use the scriptures to combat any feelings of hopelessness, anxiety, and deep sadness.

Issue	Antidote (Scripture)
If you are feeling helpless or if you need something.	Psalm 121:1-2, "I lift my eyes to the hills, where does my help come from? My help comes from The Lord, Maker of heaven and earth." Then you can say, "Lord, you are my helper. Lord my help comes from you so I will not be scared, I will not fear, you made heaven and earth and you do not sleep or get tired, so you are continuously watching over me".
You feel anxious about what is to	Matthew 6:34 Therefore do not worry about tomorrow, for tomorrow will

come next. You feel a great deal of fear about what will or will not happen.	worry about its own things. Sufficient for the day is its own trouble. Say: "I will not be worried about tomorrow. I believe that you will take care of all of my needs."
Your mind is wandering; deep thoughts of negativity.	Isaiah 26:3 "You shall keep Him in perfect peace whose mind is stayed (focused) on you, for He trusts in you." Say: "Father, I trust that You will keep my mind in perfect peace. I want to trust You with my future. Allow me to have thoughts of peace and prosperity. Help my thoughts stay focused on You." John 14:27: "Peace I leave with you, my peace I give unto you. Not as the world gives do I give to you. Let not your hearts be troubled. Neither let them be afraid." Say: "Lord Jesus Christ, I thank you for your peace. The peace you left us. Not the kind of peace the world gives. So, Lord, I receive your peace over my mind and my heart. I choose to be covered by you as I give you the issues that are causing my mind to wander"

If you are worried about not having enough. If you feel inadequate which is making you feel de-pressed or experience deep melancholy.	Philippian 4:19 19 "And my God shall supply all your needs according to His riches in glory by Christ Jesus." Say: "Father, I thank You that I do not have to be worried about provision in-side of You. You will provide for all of my needs. I choose to believe your word and I release worry, feelings of depression and anxiety to you"
If you feel afraid or fearful and anxious.	Luke 12:7, 22-32 In these verses the Lord Jesus encour-ages us to look at nature and how the Father takes care of all nature and then He asks us why we would worry since we are of more importance (value) to Him than the birds and all the other things. Say" Father, I thank you because you take care of the lilies, the birds of the air and things that are here today but gone tomorrow, like grass. Thank you that I am more important than these things. So, I release this fear and I choose to seek God's kingdom. Thank you that His kingdom has everything I need."

If you can't fall asleep because of fear or anxiety.	Psalm 4:8 "I will both lie down in peace and sleep; For You alone, Oh LORD, make me dwell in safety." Say; "My mind you can rest knowing that the Lord is the one who protects me. So, lie down in peace and rest in him"
When you are restless and having a hard time falling asleep because of a racing mind.	Take authority over your mind by saying something like this:" My mind I command you to rest. I commit everything (naming each item coming in your mind) to the Lord. Holy Spirit, please arrest my mind. Take charge of every thought, image, anything that is causing noise in my mind." Then repeat, Psalm 4: 8 "I will both lie down in peace, and sleep; for You alone, Oh Lord, make me dwell in safety"

The foregoing is just a sampling of how you can use God's Word to release peace and rid your mind of worry, anxiety, depressive thoughts and subsequently, fear. Begin to "collect" Scriptures that minister to you in a special way as you read them and add them to the list of what you use to combat troubling and disturbing thoughts.

We have looked at what CBT is. The application of Scriptural passages as CBT tools for identifying, challenging, and replacing our faulty thoughts, (also called cognitive distortions, distorted thought patterns or in more generic terms, "stinking thinking") has been demonstrated. We have reviewed that our thought patterns form what are known as core beliefs and that our core beliefs can be both positive and negative. We use CBT strategies to deal with the negative core beliefs because they are responsible for causing us to feel in ways we do not like if we do not recognize and deal with them in a timely manner. In short, Cognitive Behavioral Therapists convey that if we are feeling depressed or anxious, we must have allowed depression or anxiety causing thoughts to rule our thinking. In addition, the thoughts that need to be monitored are our automatic thoughts. These are the thoughts that come up immediately after something happens to us (event/situation or trigger). Often, these automatic thoughts tend to be negative and if we do not challenge them, we set ourselves up for the resulting behaviors, whether depression, anxiety, or fear. In this book we have shown that we can stop this by applying what the Word of God says regarding a particular situation.

As we make the habit of reading and studying God's Word on a regular basis, we will begin to replace some of our negative core beliefs and thought patterns by what His Word says about us and our situations. As that happens, we will notice that our automatic thoughts are not always negative as they used to be. We may also notice that we will start to think about ourselves in a more positive way.

Finally, remember that it takes intentionality and a willingness to learn God's Word so it can be hidden in our hearts. With memorizing and repeating scriptures, the Holy Spirit can remind us of appropriate scriptures when we need them. As mentioned earlier, please seek help from mental health professionals if your daily life is plagued with severe mental illness issues. There is ample evidence that using Scripture can help deal with mild forms of mental health issues such as depression, anxiety, and fear (Eckhardt, 2008). Therefore, I encourage every reader to believe in the power of God's word to deal with and manage anxiety and depressive symptoms.

About the Author

Joyce Nyirenda "Mama Joyce" as affectionately called by many is a Licensed Clinical Mental Health Counselor (LCMHC) and an ordained Evangelist and Elder. She has been in ministry for over 38 years and has served as lead intercessor and advisor to Warring Ministries, International for over ten years. She is a gifted preacher, teacher, writer and counselor.

Joyce enjoys her work as a counselor tremendously and uses the Word of God to help individuals overcome life's challenges. Her greatest desire is that families will gain an understanding of the importance of honoring marriage as the prime vehicle God instituted for raising families and propagating His kingdom. To this end, Joyce published her first book Preserving The Seed, in 2016.

In Bible Based Cognitive Behavioral Therapy (BB-CBT), Joyce endeavors to demonstrate how God's word can be used as an effective strategy and intervention for overcoming transient and mild depression, anxiety and fear. She combines her expertise and experience as a LCMHC and as a Christian in showing how to use the word of God for thought monitoring, challenging distorted, unhealthy thoughts, and thought replacement. She hopes that those who read this book will be helped in overcoming their depression and anxiety, which if not attended to can lead to fear and other serious mental health issues.

Joyce is a mother of four and a grandmother of three. She resides in the north Raleigh area in NC.

References

Introduction:

1. Sokol, Leslie The Comprehensive Clinician's Guide to Cognitive Behavioral Therapy. www.academyofct.org
2. Beck, A.T., Thinking and Depression: Theory and Therapy, New York, NY (1964)
3. Beck, A. T., Thinking and Depression: Theory and Therapy, New York, NY (1964)
4. Beck, A.T., Thinking and Depression: Theory and Therapy, New York, NY
5. Nimh.nih,gov/health/topics/anxiety-disorders/index.shtm/ Retrieve on 12/21/2020

Chapter 1:

6. Cognitive Behavioral Therapy for Depression CBT-D Deployment Psychology.org; Uniformed Services University (USU) Retrieved 12/21/2020
7. Sokol, Leslie., The Comprehensive Clinician's Guide to Cognitive Behavioral Therapy. www.academyofct.org
8. Nimh.nih,gov/health/topics/anxiety-disorders/index.shtm/ Retrieve on 12/21/2020
9. Sokol, Leslie. The Comprehensive Clinician's Guide to Cognitive Behavioral Therapy. www.academyofct.org

Chapter 2:

10. Meyer, Joyce. Battlefield of The Mind: Winning the Battle in Your Mind. Faithwords, 1999

Chapter 3:

11. Merriam-Webster.com. https://www.merriam-webster.com/dictionary

12. Beck, A. T., Cognitive Therapies and Emotional Disorders, New York, New American Library
13. Beck, A. T., Cognitive Therapies and Emotional Disorders, New York, New American Library.

Chapter 4:

14. Apostle Joshua Selman, Senior Pastor, Christ Gospel Church, Samaru, Zaria, Kaduna state in Nigeria.
15. Helping Children and Adolescents Cope with Violence and Disaster. ReliasLearning.com

Chapter 5:

16. Merriam-Webster.com https://www.merriam-webster.com/dictionary
17. Beck, A. T. (1976) Cognitive Therapies and Emotional Disorders, New York, New American Library
18. Signs and Symptoms of Anxiety: https://www.psychologytools.com
19. Burns, D. D. (2012); Feeling Good: The New Mood Therapy. New York; New American Library New American Library

Chapter 6:

20. The Dictionary of Psychology https://dictionary.apa.org

Chapter 7:

21. Eckhardt, J. (2008). Prayers that Rout Demons; prayers for defeating demons and overthrowing the power of darkness. Charisma House. Florida.

Made in United States
North Haven, CT
02 August 2024